ERLING HAALAND

SOCCER SUPERSTAR

BY LUKE HANLON

Copyright © 2025 by Press Room Editions. All rights reserved. No part of this book may be used or reproduced in any manner whatsoever, including internet usage, without written permission from the copyright owner, except in the case of brief quotations embodied in critical articles and reviews.

Book design by Jake Nordby
Cover design by Jake Nordby

Photographs ©: Andrew Yates/Sportimage/Cal Sport Media/AP Images, cover, 1, 25; Darren Staples/Sportimage/Cal Sport Media/AP Images, 4, 6, 30; Andrew Halseid-Budd/Getty Images Sport/Getty Images, 8, 13, 14; Christof Koepsel/Bongarts/Getty Images, 11; Andreas Schaad/Bongarts/Getty Images, 17; Jörg Schüler/Getty Images Sport/Getty Images, 19; Chris Brunskill/Fantasista/Getty Images Sport/Getty Images, 20; Harriet Lander/Copa/Getty Images Sport/Getty Images, 23; Frank Augstein/AP Images, 26–27; Red Line Editorial, 29

Press Box Books, an imprint of Press Room Editions, Inc.

ISBN
978-1-63494-951-4 (library bound)
978-1-63494-965-1 (paperback)
978-1-63494-992-7 (epub)
978-1-63494-979-8 (hosted ebook)

Library of Congress Control Number: 2024912350

Distributed by North Star Editions, Inc.
2297 Waters Drive
Mendota Heights, MN 55120
www.northstareditions.com

Printed in the United States of America
012025

About the Author
Luke Hanlon is a sportswriter and editor based in Minneapolis. He gets up early every weekend to watch Premier League matches.

TABLE OF CONTENTS

CHAPTER 1
Goal Machine 5

CHAPTER 2
Natural Athlete 9

CHAPTER 3
New League, Same Erling 15

CHAPTER 4
Winning It All 21

SPECIAL FEATURE
Celebrating in Style 26

Timeline • 28
At a Glance • 30
Glossary • 31
To Learn More • 32
Index • 32

1 GOAL MACHINE

Manchester City striker Erling Haaland started sprinting toward the goal. His teammate Jack Grealish had the ball near midfield. Grealish dribbled forward. Then he looked up and saw Haaland. The giant striker ran between two defenders. Haaland had been scoring with ease all season. And he was desperate to find the back of the net again.

Manchester City was playing against West Ham United. City was in the middle of the 2022–23 Premier League title race.

Erling Haaland had scored in five straight games before facing West Ham in 2023.

Haaland celebrates after scoring his record-breaking goal.

Meanwhile, Haaland had a chance to make history. He had scored 34 goals during his first year in the Premier League. One more and he would break the record for most goals in a season.

Grealish played a pass toward Haaland. The striker ran to the ball near the edge of the penalty area. The West Ham goalkeeper darted off his goal line. But he wasn't quick enough. Haaland calmly chipped the ball over the goalkeeper's hands. The home crowd started to roar. The ball bounced past the goal line and into the net.

Haaland slid to the ground to celebrate. His teammates quickly ran over to congratulate him. Haaland had set the Premier League on fire in his first season with City. And he showed no signs of slowing down.

EFFICIENT SCORER

Newcastle forward Andy Cole scored 34 goals in 1993–94. Blackburn Rovers forward Alan Shearer matched that number in 1994–95. Both of those players set the previous Premier League goal record in 42 games. Haaland needed only 31 games to score his 35th goal of the season.

2 NATURAL ATHLETE

Erling Haaland was born on July 21, 2000. Erling's parents grew up in Norway. However, Erling spent the first few years of his life in England. His dad, Alfie, played for English team Leeds United. Erling's dad wasn't the only athletic parent in the house. His mom, Gry, was a Norwegian champion in track and field.

The family didn't stay in England for long. Alfie played three seasons for Leeds United. He then spent three years with

Erling Haaland started playing professionally in 2016.

Manchester City before retiring from soccer. After that, the family moved to Bryne, Norway. That city is where both Alfie and Gry grew up. They wanted to raise Erling there, too.

Erling's parents gifted him with elite athleticism. As a kid, Erling thrived in multiple sports. He played handball and golf. Like Gry, he competed in track and field. When he was five, Erling performed a standing jump of 1.63 meters (5 feet, 4 inches). That set a world record for five-year-olds. But Erling always loved soccer the most.

Erling began playing soccer when he was five. He said he dreamed of being like his dad. Just playing professionally wasn't enough for Erling, though. He wanted to be better than Alfie. He planned to become one of the best players in the world.

Erling Haaland's height allowed him to score lots of headers.

Alfie had mostly played as a midfielder. However, Erling played as a forward. Scoring goals came naturally to him. When Erling was five, a Norwegian coach watched him play. The first two times Erling touched the ball, he set up two goals.

Erling's soccer career started in his hometown. He played for Bryne's youth academy. Coaches thought Erling was too good to play against kids his own age. So, they put him with kids who were a year older. Playing against bigger kids helped Erling. He had to learn how to score goals while being smaller and weaker than his opponents.

At 15, Erling made his professional debut with Bryne's senior team. He played only 16 games for the team. Then Molde came calling. Molde is one of the top clubs in Norway. The team's coach thought Erling

LOYAL TO NORWAY

Erling Haaland started his international career with Norway's youth team. Since he was born in Leeds, he could have played for England's senior team. But Erling decided to play for Norway instead. He had only lived in England until he was three. Erling said playing for Norway felt more natural to him.

Molde finished second in Norway's top soccer league in Erling Haaland's first season there.

was ready for the challenge. Erling signed with the team in February 2017. He played his first game for Molde two months later. He scored the team's first goal to help Molde win 3–2. The goals kept coming from there.

3 NEW LEAGUE, SAME ERLING

Erling Haaland scored four goals in his first season with Molde. He earned more playing time in his second season. Soon, more goals followed. Molde played against Brann on July 1, 2018. Brann was in first place in the Norwegian league. A 17-year-old Erling scored a goal less than four minutes into the game. By the 21st minute, he had scored three more. Erling's heroics lifted Molde to a 4–0 win.

Haaland finished the 2018 season as Molde's leading scorer. He received

Haaland recorded 20 goals and six assists in 50 games with Molde.

NEVER SATISFIED

Erling Haaland played for Norway at the 2019 Under-20 World Cup. Norway faced Honduras in a group stage game. Haaland scored four goals in the first half. One of his teammates said Haaland was mad in the locker room. He couldn't stop thinking about a scoring chance that he'd missed. In the second half, Haaland tallied five more goals.

the Norwegian league's Breakthrough Athlete of the Year Award for his play. During the season, other European teams scouted Haaland. They were impressed by his size, strength, and speed. Multiple teams tried to sign him. That included his father's old team Leeds United. But Haaland decided not to play in England. Instead, he signed with Red Bull Salzburg in Austria.

RB Salzburg were the champions of the Austrian league. Winning the league meant RB Salzburg got to play in the Champions League. That is a competition between the top teams

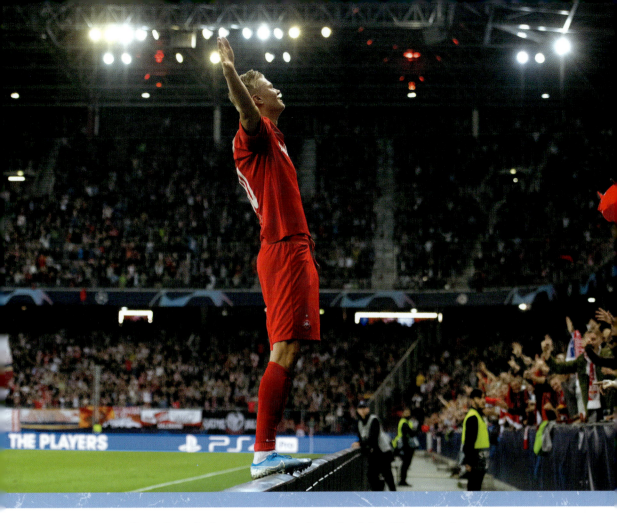

Haaland celebrates scoring in his Champions League debut.

in Europe. Haaland's first Champions League game came in September 2019. RB Salzburg faced Genk, the Belgian champions. Playing on a big stage didn't scare Haaland. He opened the scoring in the second minute of the game.

By halftime, he had tallied a hat trick. He became the first player in history to score a first-half hat trick in a Champions League debut.

Haaland seemed to step up his game in the Champions League. He scored against English team Liverpool. Then he netted two goals against Italian team Napoli. Haaland ended up scoring a goal in each of his first five Champions League games. He became only the third player in history to do that.

Haaland's run of goals caught the attention of bigger European teams. Borussia Dortmund was one of them. The German team signed Haaland near the end of December 2019. The young star continued his hot scoring run in a tougher league. Haaland came off the bench for his Dortmund debut. It took him only 20 minutes to record a hat trick. He then scored

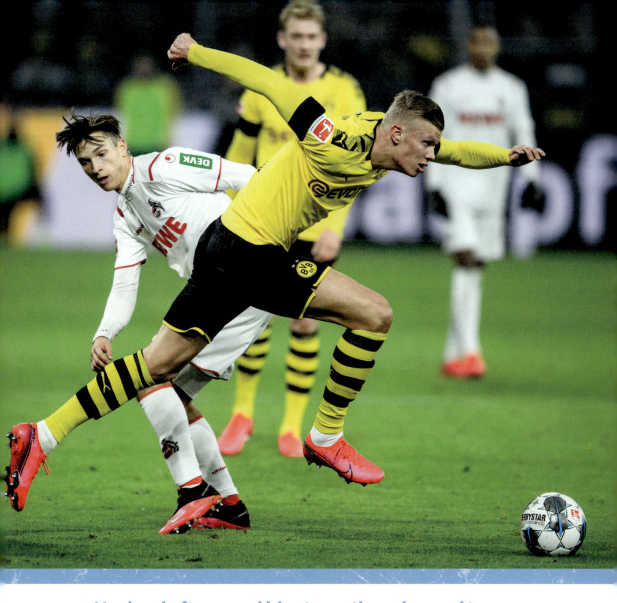

Haaland often used his strength and speed to glide past defenders.

two goals in each of his next two games. No matter what league he played in, Haaland always seemed to find a way to score.

4 WINNING IT ALL

In February 2020, Erling Haaland played in his first Champions League game for Borussia Dortmund. It came against Paris Saint-Germain, the French champions. Haaland tallied the game's opening goal in the 69th minute. In the 77th minute, he rifled a shot from outside the penalty area. It found the back of the net and helped secure a Dortmund win.

Haaland routinely showed up on big occasions for Dortmund. In 2021, Dortmund reached the final of the

In 89 games for Dortmund, Haaland recorded 86 goals and 23 assists.

DFB-Pokal. That is the top cup competition in Germany. Haaland netted two goals to win his first trophy for Dortmund.

After the 2021–22 season, Haaland decided to leave Dortmund. Still only 21 years old, he was one of the most valuable players in the world. Manchester City won the race to sign him.

City was coming off two straight Premier League titles when it signed Haaland. The Premier League is the top soccer league in England. Now the powerhouse club had one of the world's best strikers. However, some experts thought Haaland didn't fit into City's playing style. Others thought he would struggle to score in the Premier League. Playing in new leagues had never slowed down Haaland before. And it took him almost no time to

Haaland uses his preferred left foot to score in his debut for Manchester City.

silence those doubts. His first Premier League game came against West Ham. Haaland scored twice to lift City to a 2–0 win.

Haaland recorded his first Premier League hat trick in his fourth game for City. Four days later, he scored another hat trick. Any worry about Haaland adjusting to the Premier League had faded. He finished the season with a record 36 goals.

Haaland's goals lifted City to another Premier League title. Then the team won the FA Cup. That is the top cup competition in England. All that remained for City was the Champions League. However, the club had never won that tournament before. Signing Haaland helped change that. The striker scored 12 goals in 11 Champions League games in 2022-23. City then defeated Italian team Inter Milan 1-0 in the final to become champions of Europe.

STAYING ZEN

Erling Haaland sometimes meditates. It helps him clear his mind from the stresses of being a pro athlete. Meditating also has inspired his signature goal celebration. After scoring, Haaland sometimes sits with his legs crossed to look like he's meditating.

Haaland connects with a header to score against Manchester United in a 2023 game.

Haaland kept rolling during the 2023–24 season. He once again finished as the Premier League's top scorer. And he helped City win the league for the fourth year in a row. No team had ever won four first-division English league titles in a row before. With Haaland leading the attack, City seemed almost unstoppable.

CELEBRATING IN STYLE

Erling Haaland earned his team a penalty kick during his Premier League debut. He took the penalty and scored his first goal for City. After scoring, Haaland showcased his signature meditating celebration.

TIMELINE

1. Leeds, England (July 21, 2000)
Erling Haaland is born.

2. Volda, Norway (April 26, 2017)
Erling scores a goal in his debut for Molde.

3. Lublin, Poland (May 30, 2019)
Playing against Honduras in the Under-20 World Cup, Haaland scores nine goals in a 12–0 win.

4. Salzburg, Austria (September 17, 2019)
Haaland tallies a first-half hat trick in his first Champions League game.

5. Berlin, Germany (May 13, 2021)
Haaland scores two goals and lifts Borussia Dortmund to the DFB-Pokal championship.

6. London, England (August 7, 2022)
In his Premier League debut, Haaland scores both goals in a 2–0 Manchester City win.

7. Manchester, England (May 3, 2023)
Haaland scores his 35th goal of the season, setting a Premier League record for most goals in a single season.

8. Istanbul, Turkey (June 10, 2023)
Haaland and Manchester City win the 2023 Champions League title.

MAP

29

AT A GLANCE

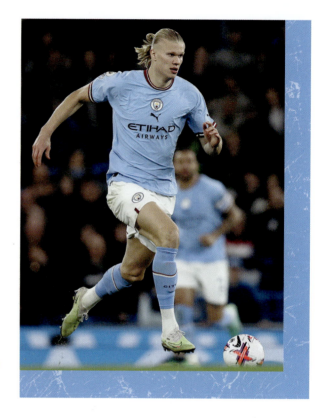

Birth date: July 21, 2000

Birthplace: Leeds, England

Position: Striker

Preferred foot: Left

Size: 6-foot-3 (191 cm), 192 pounds (87 kg)

Current team: Manchester City (2022–)

Previous teams: Bryne (2016), Molde (2017–18), Red Bull Salzburg (2019), Borussia Dortmund (2020–22)

Major awards: Eliteserien Breakthrough Athlete of the Year (2018), PFA Player of the Year (2023), Premier League Golden Boot (2023, 2024)

Accurate through the 2023–24 season.

GLOSSARY

debut
First appearance.

elite
The best of the best.

group stage
The first part of a tournament where teams are divided into small groups. Each team plays every team in its group, and the teams with the best records advance.

hat trick
When a player scores three or more goals in a game.

penalty area
The 18-yard box in front of the goal where a player is granted a penalty kick if he or she is fouled.

penalty kick
A kick taken 12 yards away from the goal. The kick is usually awarded after a foul in the penalty box. It is also used to settle a tied match.

professionally
Paid to do something as a job.

striker
A forward whose main job is to score goals.

TO LEARN MORE

Books

Hanlon, Luke. *The Best Men's Players of World Soccer*. Minneapolis: Abdo Publishing, 2024.

Jökulsson, Illugi. *Stars of World Soccer: Fourth Edition*. New York: Abbeville Press, 2023.

Leed, Percy. *Pro Soccer by the Numbers*. Minneapolis: Lerner Publications, 2025.

More Information

To learn more about Erling Haaland, go to **pressboxbooks.com/AllAccess.**

These links are routinely monitored and updated to provide the most current information available.

INDEX

Blackburn Rovers, 7
Brann, 15

Cole, Andy, 7

Genk, 17
Grealish, Jack, 5, 7

Inter Milan, 24

Leeds United, 9, 16
Liverpool, 18

Napoli, 18
Newcastle, 7

Paris Saint-Germain, 21

Shearer, Alan, 7

West Ham United, 5, 7, 23